A SHORT WALK AROUND THE PYRAMIDS
& THROUGH THE WORLD OF ART

A Short Walk Around the Pyramids
& Through the World of Art

BY PHILIP M. ISAACSON

EMBER

FOR DEBORAH

I would not have embarked on this
adventure without the encouragement
of my editor, Stephanie Spinner.
For her advice and gentle badgering,
I am more grateful than I can say.

Visit us on the Web! randomhouseteens.com

Educators and librarians, for a variety of teaching tools,
visit us at RHTeachersLibrarians.com

The Library of Congress has cataloged the hardcover
edition of this work as follows:
Isaacson, Philip M., 1924–2013
A short walk around the Pyramids & through the world of
art. by Philip M. Isaacson.
p. cm.
Summary: Introduces tangible and abstract components
of art, and the many forms art can take including
sculpture, pottery, painting, photographs, and even
furniture and cities.
ISBN 978-0-679-81523-5 (trade) —
ISBN 978-0-679-91523-2 (lib. bdg.)
1. Art—Juvenile literature. [1. Art.] I. Title.
N7440.I8 1993 91-8854 700—dc20

ISBN 978-0-553-53550-1 (tr. pbk.)

Photograph credits follow the index.

MANUFACTURED IN MALAYSIA
10 9 8 7 6 5 4 3 2 1

First Ember Edition 2015

Frontispiece | This is a photograph of one of the wonders
of ancient Egypt, the pyramid complex of Zoser. The
sand plain in the foreground is called the Great Court.
It leads to the Step Pyramid, the oldest of all of Egypt's
magnificent structures.

CONTENTS

A SHORT WALK AROUND THE PYRAMIDS
& THROUGH THE WORLD OF ART

A SIMPLE FORM

This is a place called Saqqara (1). It is on the edge of a great desert an hour's drive from Cairo. You could reach it by camel, but that would take much longer. As you approach Saqqara, a line of walls and a strange pyramid rise from the sand like a golden mirage. But they are not a mirage. They are among the oldest works of art in the world. They were built more than

CHAPTER ONE

2

4,600 years ago by an Egyptian king with a wonderful imagination. His name was Zoser.

The pyramid that came from Zoser's imagination—with help from his architect, Imhotep—is called the Step Pyramid (2). It is made of pieces of stone stacked to form six huge steps. Its sides were once covered by a layer of white limestone that transformed it into a star, dazzling in the pure desert air. The Step Pyramid was the first pyramid ever built. Although it is such a simple, logical shape, no one before Zoser and Imhotep had ever thought of it, and when it was finished, those steps climbing high above the desert must have caused hearts to jump with surprise and fear. They still do.

The Step Pyramid, which may have been King Zoser's tomb, inspired other Egyptian rulers to build even larger pyramids. At Giza, a few miles north of Saqqara, sit three great pyramids, each named for the king—or Pharaoh—during whose reign it was built. No other buildings are so well known, yet the first sight of them sitting in their field is breathtaking. When you walk among them, you walk in a place made for giants. They seem too large to have been made by human beings, too perfect to have been formed by nature, and, when the sun is overhead, not solid enough to be attached to the sand (3). In the

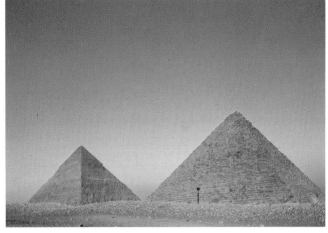

3

4

minutes before sunrise, they are the color of faded roses (4), and when the last rays of the desert sun touch them, they turn to amber (5). But whatever the light, their broad proportions, the beauty of the limestone, and the care with which it is fitted into place create three unforgettable works of art.

What do we learn about art when we look at the pyramids?

First, when all of the things that go into a work—its components—complement one another, they create an object that has a certain spirit, and we can call that spirit *harmony*. The pyramids are harmonious because limestone, a warm, quiet material, is a cordial companion for a simple, logical, and pleasing shape. In fact, the stone and the shape are so comfortable with each other that the pyramids seem inevitable—as though they were bound to have exactly the form, color, and texture that they do have.

5

The pyramids also show us that simple things must be made with care. The fine workmanship that went into the building of the pyramids is a part of their beauty. Complicated shapes may conceal poor work—such shapes distract our eye—but in something as simple as a pyramid, there is no way to hide flaws. Because any flaw would mar its beauty, the craftsmanship must be perfect.

Look at a recent pyramid (6). It is made of glass and was finished in 1989. Designed by an American architect, I. M. Pei, it is in the Cour Napoléon, one of the great courtyards of the Louvre Palace in Paris. The Louvre is a famous museum, and the pyramid is its new entrance. It is a pure crystal, bending the light of Paris into silver, pale blue, and yellow and multiplying

6

7

itself in the pools around it. Any building less beautifully designed or made with less skill would have looked awkward in the company of the dignified old structures near it.

Finally, pyramids show us that light helps to shape our feelings about art. As the sun moves above the desert, the pyramids seem to change. As they do, our feelings about them also change. In the early morning they sit squarely on the horizon, and we feel that they have become the kings after whom they are named (7); by midday they have become restless and change into silver-white clouds (8); and at dusk they settle down and regain their power.

The pyramids will always work their magic on us. Their forms, so simple and reasonable, and their great size lift us high above the ordinary moments in our lives.

8

9

SCULPTURE

As we have seen, art does not have to be complicated to be wonderful. Still, art can be more complicated, often much more complicated, than the pyramids at Saqqara and Giza.

We are looking at a piece of sculpture—the head of a horse carved in marble the color of cream (9). But it's more than a horse. It

CHAPTER TWO

10

represents the Greek goddess of the moon, Selene, as she drops from the night into a dark sea (10). The horse was carved about 435 B.C. for a temple on a hill in the ancient city of Athens.

The temple is called the Parthenon (11), and the horse was part of a group of figures made especially for its east pediment, a large stone triangle fitted just under the roof. The Parthenon, high on a hill, catches the first light of morning. The carvers wanted the sight of that golden light washing across the horse and a line of other gods to be unforgettable. And so they coaxed the images of their gods out of the marble with such tenderness that they gave the world an example of ideal beauty. Each figure is as calm and as refined as our minds can imagine. They are so noble and quiet that they do seem godly and perfect companions for the noble, quiet temple.

If you visit Athens, you will not find the Horse of Selene or its neighbors. They were taken from

11

12

the Parthenon early in the nineteenth century, shipped to London, and placed in the British Museum. And they were given a new name, the Elgin Marbles, after Lord Elgin, the man who brought them to England. Those marble shapes, even though they are now battered and broken, weave a spell around everyone who comes to them (12).

In their still room in the museum, we can see how beautifully they are carved. The jowls of the horse, its muzzle, the backs of the other gods — all things that could not have been seen when they were on their high perch — are cut with as much care as though they had been made for the floor of the great temple (13, 14). By making their work so perfect, the sculptors expressed their devotion to the goddess Athena, to whom the Parthenon was dedicated. Throughout the ages much of art has been created to express deep spiritual feelings. As acts of devotion and honor

13

14

they add an essential ingredient to art—emotion. Without emotion, even the most harmonious work will not truly stir us.

This piece of sculpture (15) is very different from ancient Greek carving, though it, too, is part of an old religious tradition. It is made of hard wood covered with small plates of brass and copper and comes from Gabon, a West African country that straddles the equator. It was made by the Kota, a group of tribes who worship in similar ways, and who have made figures such as this for a hundred years, and probably much longer.

In the past, the Kota spoke to the bones of their ancestors before making important decisions. They stored the bones in small baskets woven of rolls of bark or leaves. Sculpture such as this piece—which is called a Kota funerary figure—was tied to the top of the baskets. We are not certain what the figure meant to the Kota.

15

Perhaps it was magical, a figure that possessed power and could help in some way when help was needed. Or perhaps it was something quite different. We may never know the answer, for the Kota, like many of the tribes of Africa, have changed their old ways, and the meaning of many of their traditions has been lost.

If we knew more about the old customs of the Kota, our experience would be richer, but whatever its original meaning, the Kota funerary figure is still a powerful work of art. It can reach across a hundred years and a language we don't understand to touch our lives. We recognize the figure as a person, although it doesn't look like one. Instead of copying the human body—and many African tribes could do that perfectly—it only suggests the human body. It excites our imagination, and our imagination turns the Kota figure into a person. Its triangles, cylinders, and parts of circles remind us of eyes, a neck, and hair, and our imagination tells us that we are looking at a human figure. The figure is an example of abstract art, an art that doesn't intend things to look real. If we searched, we could find examples of abstract art the world over.

The traditional art of African nations is a wonderful part of the world's art. Like the art of all people who live in groups called tribes—the people of the Pacific islands, the Native Americans (16), the Eskimos, the Indians of the Northwest Coast of Canada—it was once called primitive art. But it isn't primitive. It isn't primitive in its shape or in the way it is made or in the deep feelings it expresses. There doesn't seem to be a good short name for the traditional art of tribal societies, but that's not important. We should enjoy it, as we enjoy all art, because of its form, its color, its materials, and its beautiful workmanship, and for what we may know of the people who made it.

16

17

This bronze sculpture stands in the courtyard of the Hirshhorn Museum in Washington, D.C. (17). It is the work of a sculptor named Jacques Lipchitz and was made in the years 1926–30. Because it is bronze, it wasn't carved. Instead, the artist shaped it in plaster. The plaster was taken to a foundry, where a mold was made from it. Molten bronze was then poured into the mold, and when it cooled and was opened, *Figure,* as the work is called, emerged. *Figure*'s form and spirit are much like the Kota piece. Both are powerful and abstract and remind us of the human body. They have concave faces and hypnotic eyes, and are pierced by holes that suggest parts of the human body. *Figure* couldn't look the way it does if the artists of Gabon had not made their funerary figures first. The Lipchitz sculpture and the Kota funerary figure teach us that the art of one people or of one time may influence the art of other peoples and times.

This is another bronze sculpture (18), and it is also in a museum. Called *Knife Edge Mirror Two Piece,* it is a huge work by the British sculptor Henry Moore and stands at the entry of the East Building of the National Gallery of Art in Washington, D.C. It is even more abstract than *Figure* because it doesn't suggest any one thing that we have seen in the world. Still, its smooth surface, its soft sheen, and its curves flowing easily into one another remind us of something that we've seen in nature. Perhaps it is the graceful spirit of things that grow, of movement, of the gentle part of the natural world.

18

19

This is also sculpture (19), but it is very different from the pieces we have seen. We can't walk around it to look at its sides or its back, for it has none. Like a drawing, it has only a front, one that barely lifts itself above its flat background. It is called low-relief, or bas-relief, sculpture. Rather than having three-dimensional form, it suggests it. Its shallow surfaces give us hints about the human body, and from those hints we complete the figure in our mind. Through tiny shadows and thin strokes of light, a bowed, elderly man rises from a dark field. In this quiet, dignified work, called *Homage to Augustus Saint-Gaudens,* one American artist, Leonard Baskin, salutes another. Baskin chose low relief to tell us that Saint-Gaudens was himself a master of relief sculpture.

This is part of the Shaw Memorial (20). The memorial was finished by Saint-Gaudens in 1897, after fourteen years of work, and placed on the edge of the Boston Common (21). It describes the pride and courage of the 54th Massachusetts Colored Volunteer Infantry Regiment during the Civil War. Because its commander, Colonel Robert Gould Shaw, and the soldiers who were killed with him in battle were devoted to the same cause, Saint-Gaudens saw them as one force. Each is a separate person, yet in the way they march—locked together— and in the look on their faces—conviction and courage—he tied them to one another forever.

20

Most of the things that we have considered so far have three dimensions: height, width, and thickness. They have been buildings and sculpture, solid things that we can reach out and touch. Some are very simple forms. Others are more complicated. Sculpture that doesn't look real we called *abstract* and said it sometimes stood for things that we can see and sometimes for things we can only sense. All that we have seen has given us a sense of harmony and has touched our emotions. We found harmony when design, materials, and craftsmanship joined to become an agreeable whole. And we learned that harmony alone does not make a wonderful work of art. Art must also stir our emotions, and it can do this in many ways. The three great pyramids did this through their colossal size and their dramatic seat on the edge of a desert. The Elgin Marbles and the Kota figure achieved it by carrying the deep spiritual feelings of their artists to us.

22

COLOR

This is a mobile (22). Its slim rods and simple forms are so delicately balanced that even a passing breeze will make it tremble. And when the mobile runs with the breeze, the forms twist and spin, cutting circles within circles in the air. To this graceful performance the mobile's maker, Alexander Calder, added a lively touch—color. Up to now, in looking at sculpture, our thoughts have only been about form. The mobile gives us the opportunity to think about color.

It's not difficult to do so with a mobile. When it's at rest, it is a thin outline, almost a drawing, floating above our heads. When it stirs, its parts set out on many paths, and to help us follow them, some of its parts have been painted a bright color (23). Calder often used red, yellow, and blue because they are strong and clear, much like the forms in the mobile. And, of course, strong colors spinning in the sky are exciting.

Now let's look at color in a painting. This is by a Dutch artist named Piet Mondrian and is called *Broadway Boogie-Woogie* (24). It doesn't tell us what Broadway actually looked like in 1943, the year it was painted, but it does tell us how the painter felt about that famous part of Manhattan. As we can see, it delighted him. He found it throbbing with energy. In the painting it is

23

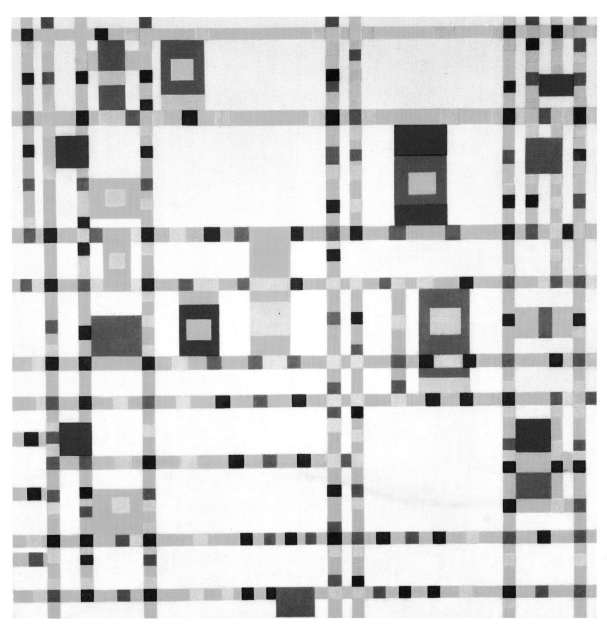

24

nighttime, and we can imagine streams of taxis lighting up the streets, electric signs blinking on and off, and the windows of skyscrapers forming checkered curtains of yellow light.

Like Alexander Calder, Piet Mondrian used red, yellow, and blue: the strong primary colors. Yellow, the liveliest, seems to grow as we look at it—and so quickly that it almost runs off the canvas. The blue is bright, but feels cool. Instead of growing, it appears to shrink, and so, with the help of dull gray, it calms the ribbons of yellow by breaking them into short strips.

And then there's the red. It is warm and deep, and its task is to warm our feelings about Manhattan at night. Finally, there's the white. It is a bystander. Its task is to provide a quiet background that encourages the other colors.

In *Broadway Boogie-Woogie,* color makes us think of movement, and by suggesting straight streets and walls of lighted windows, it helps to build form. But color can play many other roles. For example, there were times when color was used because of what it stood for. In ancient Rome, purple represented the emperor, and in old religious art, white stood for purity and blue for the quiet beauty of love. Let's look at some of the roles that artists, over the years, have selected for color.

25

The artist who painted this portrait (25) was well known over five hundred years ago. His name was Andrea del Castagno and he lived in Florence, Italy. We no longer know the name of the gentleman who posed for the portrait, but we're certain that he was an influential person. What gives us that feeling? The answer lies in the color of the cloak. The red is so deep and powerful that it almost glows. Its boldness gives the man an aura of importance, of power. Would he be as impressive if he were wearing a restful color, such as blue or green? Probably not.

What's the first thing that we notice in this famous picture (26)? The red hat, of course, and the picture is actually called *The Girl with the Red Hat*. It was painted about 350 years ago by the Dutch artist Jan Vermeer. That hat is fascinating. Its top is so soaked with light that the young woman appears to be wearing a tray of sunshine. And the brilliant red comes as a fresh surprise each time that we see it.

26

The great American artist Thomas Eakins completed this portrait (27) in 1874. Its title is *John Biglin in a Single Scull*. In the 1870s John Biglin and his brother Bernard were well-known professional oarsmen, and Eakins often painted them. To attract our attention, Eakins painted the scull a deep red, and to emphasize John Biglin's strength, he used an even brighter red for the kerchief. That bit of clothing draws our eyes toward the tense muscles in Biglin's back and arms.

28

In these three portraits we've found that a single color—red—can stir us by suggesting power, surprise, or strength. But not all colors have the power to excite; some, such as those in *Still Life—Siena Rose* by William Bailey (28), bring quiet pleasure. In this still-life painting, the artist has created a world so hushed that its stillness is as much a part of the picture as the things in it. Built with quiet tones by Bailey's brush, objects that we might find in our homes are transformed into an imaginary landscape, a silent town constructed according to his ideas about color, texture, and shape. By the way, the title is a pun. It tells us that the artist was inspired by Siena, a town on a lonely Italian hilltop, and by sienna, the pigment that gives both the old town and his painting their earthy color.

This is a portrait of the American artist
Marsden Hartley (29), and it was painted in
1943 by his friend Milton Avery. At first, the
colors in it seem strange. Hartley couldn't have
had a lime green face and probably did not wear
purple and raspberry clothing. The painter chose
these colors for several reasons. For one thing,
they tell us how he felt about his friend. The
beautiful colors in the clothing suggest that
Hartley had an artistic nature, but the green face
and startling blue eyes hint at something sad in
that nature. But more than this, we can see that
Milton Avery simply enjoyed the beauty of color.
He used it to do more than build form; he
allowed it to have a life of its own, a life that is
not part of the world we see, but rather one that
began in his dreams and imagination.

29

Of course, many other artists have used color to express their imagination. Paul Gauguin, a French artist, is one of the most famous of them. He painted *Fatata te Miti* (30) in 1892. (In Polynesian, the title means *By the Sea.*) In this magnificent painting we see a tropical world that is impossibly beautiful. The colors, which are richer and deeper than those found in nature, bump pleasantly against one another. They form large patterns—purples, oranges, greens, and browns—and each pattern is an independent world. Each is a place of intense, complicated color, and yet these neighbors fit together to form a masterpiece.

31

This view of an old palace on the choppy Grand Canal (31) is called *Palazzo da Mula, Venice* and was painted by Claude Monet in the winter of 1908. It's very different from the imaginary paradise painted by Paul Gauguin. There are no bold patterns in it, and its colors are neither very dark nor very light. But as we study the picture, we see that color creeps in on the back of the winter light to form windows, doorways, and balconies. Rather than dissolving the building, color actually shapes it. Color builds form, but it also makes us think about light and how quickly it can change. In his *The Houses of Parliament, Sunset* (32), Monet took the haze from a pink and yellow sky, and by adding blue and green fashioned a line of towers that dye the waters of the Thames. Monet spent his life studying light in every time and season, and his radiant, light-filled paintings, especially those of his native France, have charmed the world.

33

This scene is also in Venice (33). It's of a canal called the Cannaregio. It was painted in about 1770 by a Venetian painter named Francesco Guardi. If we look at it quickly, the busy scene is not at all like Monet's picture of the lonely palace on the canal. But if we take our time, we see that it too is a study of light. Like Claude Monet, Francesco Guardi was fascinated by the way changes in light bring changes in color. The sun is setting, the shadows are growing long, and the colors are changing quickly. For the moment, the light is delicately touched with gold, and Guardi, in *View on the Cannaregio, Venice,* has reached out, caught the light, and then used it to soften the stones of that gnarled old city. *A Seaport and Classic Ruins in Italy* (34), unlike the *Cannaregio,* is not a picture of a particular place. It is an imaginary scene taken by Guardi from bits and pieces of old Roman and Italian buildings, but, as in the *Cannaregio*, light polishes its forms.

34

35

IMAGES

This is a sublime moment (35). We are back in 1862, standing along the shore of a small island in Penobscot Bay, Maine. Ahead of us is a finger of land called Owl's Head, and beyond, in the distance, are the Camden Hills. It is sunset. Light, like a phantom, slides across the bay, tracing the edges of all that it touches. The still ship, the man leaning on the pole, the line of houses are locked in that light-filled moment. Does it look real? Yes, but somehow it isn't quite what we have seen in nature. The water, the high clouds, the reflections are familiar; still, we have a feeling that they, the ship, the boatman in his red shirt, the stillness, and the pure light are so perfect that the moment could never have happened. We have a feeling that it is partly an illusion.

We have been looking at a painting by Fitz Hugh Lane. It is called *Owl's Head,* and it is one of many that he painted of the same scene. In his imagination, Lane saw the bay as an enchanted place, and he painted it according to that private vision. He moved the Camden Hills from their true location (far to the right of the lighthouse); he lowered the Head a bit; and he put in a square-sailed vessel and a boatman. And he joined all of this together by a light that is so clear, so weightless, that it is magical.

Therefore, although Lane's scene—a landscape—is beautiful, it isn't really what he saw from that island. It's what he saw in his imagination. Like the carvers of the Elgin Marbles (12), he has given us something idealized. *Owl's Head* is another reminder that artists invent and change forms to express their imagination and their feelings.

In this painting we're still on the Maine coast, but on an island called Vinalhaven (36). It is about the year 1938, and instead of a quiet, light-washed bay, we find granite and dark water. Black pines notch the sky, and they, the rocks, and the water seem roughly painted, almost crude. The painting is called *After the Storm, Vinalhaven*. In it, painter Marsden Hartley (whose portrait we saw on page 39) describes his feelings about a place made of hard granite, near a sea that is often unfriendly. Unlike *Owl's Head,* this painting doesn't look at all real; still, through its raw, powerfully painted forms and its simple, vivid colors, we sense the stern character of that rugged island.

So we see that two artists may have quite different feelings about a similar place. One, Fitz Hugh Lane, is moved by the calm, quiet side of nature; the other, Marsden Hartley, by its dramatic side. Both artists tell us about their

36

feelings, and although one painting is more realistic than the other, neither copies nature. Through a delicate wash of light, Lane shows us a moment that never quite happened in a place that seems quite real; through simple, rugged shapes, Hartley tells us about the rough power in the natural world and, perhaps, in himself.

This is our third landscape (37). It was painted by April Gornik, and its title is *Fresh Light.* In it, the field, the trees around it, and the sky are softened by damp summer light. The light gives the painting an air of emptiness, as though no one has ever walked in this lonely place. *Fresh Light* is not like *Owl's Head* or *After the Storm, Vinalhaven.* We're certain that each of those places exist. In *Fresh Light* we're not so certain, and its painter doesn't give us the answer; she provides us with a glimpse of a soft moment in nature and then asks us to decide the question for ourselves.

38

Does this place exist (38)? Before we try to answer, we must decide what we're looking at. It's a painting by Ellen Phelan and is called *After Atget*. "Atget" refers to Eugène Atget, a photographer who lived in Paris and who, from about 1900 to 1927, produced carefully composed photographs taken along country roads in France and in the streets of Paris (39). Ellen Phelan admires them. Her painting was probably inspired by one of Atget's photographs of an old French road. It is almost entirely abstract; still, in its dancing planes of color we can find forms that remind us of a road, trees, and the bright, wet sunshine that follows a rain. The landscape doesn't look real, but the forms are so bold that we feel that such a place must exist. The forms are only hints, but we accept them—and with them the reality of the place.

39

40

This is a painting (40) by Frank Stella and it is even more abstract than *After Atget.* In that painting, with the help of our imagination, we could find the road and follow it through the trees and into the distance. Here there is no distance. Instead of being able to look into a scene, our eyes stop at the face of the canvas.

Up to now we have used paintings as windows to peer into a story. We cannot do that with this work because its flat bands of color do not lead our eye beyond the surface of the canvas, and its unusual shape even reminds us of sculpture. Can we find a story in its stiff forms? Perhaps they suggest a place, much as the Kota figure (15) suggested the human body.

The title, *Chocorua II,* gives us a hint. Chocorua is the name of a pyramid-shaped mountain rising amid the lakes in eastern New Hampshire. Nearby is the Saco River, and beyond the river is the dark Pemigewasset Wilderness. Knowing this, we can find symbols that remind us of a triangular peak, a fast-moving yellow river, and, finally, a deep green wilderness. Like the forms in all of the paintings that we have looked at in this chapter, the symbols in *Chocorua II* join to give us the feeling of a landscape.

Will we always be able to find a story in paintings? Perhaps not. There are many reasons for creating art, and telling a story is only one of them. For example, an artist can paint simply to express feelings or just for the pleasure of painting, without describing something exactly.

Look at this painting by Jackson Pollock (41). Its name, *Composition with Pouring II,* tells us that it was made by pouring and perhaps by spattering paint on a canvas. It has no story to relate other than that of the many complicated routes the painter's hand took as he created the work. In following the trails on the face of *Composition,* we feel close to the very act of painting. They make us feel that Pollock is still near the picture and that we are near to him.

So we must learn to enjoy some paintings for the feelings created by their forms and colors alone. We were able to do this with the pyramids at Saqqara and Giza (1–5; 7, 8), and when we have come to do this with paintings, we will find that this is an important part of the pleasure that art can bring to us.

42

PHOTOGRAPHS

This famous photograph (42) is called *Fifth Avenue Houses, Nos. 4, 6 and 8, New York, 1936*. It was made by Berenice Abbott, a distinguished photographer. The photograph describes an ordinary event, yet it is a great achievement. A man crosses the avenue; behind him is a row of stone houses caught in a moment that will last forever. For that instant they become solemn, brooding forms that dominate the world around them. Suddenly they are more than houses on Fifth Avenue; they are revelations about the power of simple forms to move us deeply.

Is this a work of art? Of course it is. Forms that begin as deep, velvety blacks, move smoothly across a range of grays, and finally blend into delicate whites are wonderfully harmonious, and the composition—the way the man, the truck, and the buildings are arranged—is full of tension. The man, the truck, and the houses are a triangle of forms that are forever trying to move away from one another and forever being tugged back.

Looking at a photograph such as this, it is difficult to believe that although photography is nearly 200 years old, during most of that time it wasn't thought of as art. A photographer can make about as many good prints of an image as he or she wishes. For years this seemed odd to many painters and sculptors. They felt that a work of art should be unique, that there should be only one of it, or, at most, a few copies. They also felt that art had to be made with brushes or, perhaps, carving tools—and not by a machine. Finally, many artists felt that a camera only copied what the photographer saw; that, like a mirror, it simply reflected nature.

However, we now recognize that being able to produce prints for many people to enjoy is a special quality. And we know that a camera can be used to create images that move us deeply and are often different from what we see in nature.

Look at these theological students twirling in a snowstorm (43). Why are they out there, and what kind of game are they playing? Why are some of the figures so distorted that they are ghostlike, almost frightening? Why are parts of the photograph, which is called *Pretini 63,* clear, while other parts are so fuzzy that they are hard to understand? If we were to ask these questions of Mario Giacomelli, the Italian photographer who made this haunting image, he might tell us that he is fascinated by the world of imagination and dreams. By bending and scratching his negatives and seeking out odd moments in the lives of people, Giacomelli makes photographic prints that describe his fantasies to us. Through photography he takes us beyond what is real, into the private world of his dreams.

43

Or look at *Dancing Nightly* (44), a color photograph made in 1941 by Harry Callahan. In it the photographer expresses his feelings about jitterbugging, the fast, acrobatic dancing of the time. Like a jitterbugging dancer, the image of a Detroit nightclub bobs, twists, and goes into wild swings. We can't see much of the building, but by moving his camera about and making multiple exposures of its hotly colored signs, Callahan gives us a sense that the building is spinning through the night. Rather than describe the building to us, he describes the spirit of a popular dance by making his work abstract.

The lens in the camera, the way the camera is handled, the way the camera admits light, the kind of film used, and the way the picture is processed allow photographers to give their pictures almost any appearance they wish them to have. A photographer does not have as much freedom to adjust forms and colors as a painter,

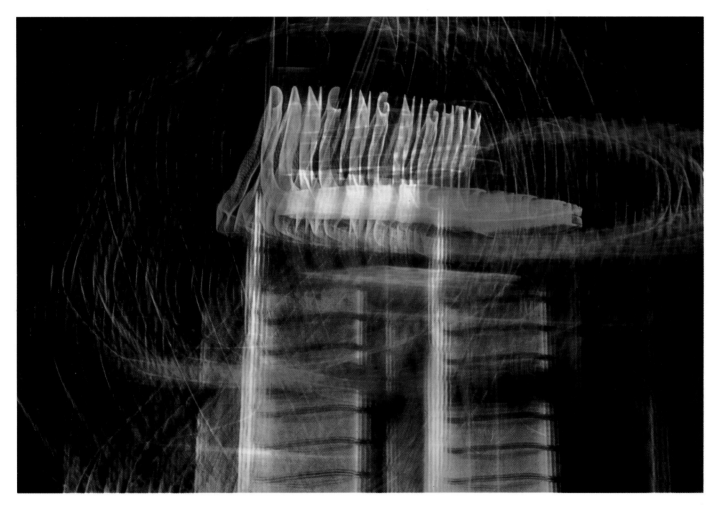

44

but when the photographer is moved by a wonderful image and uses a camera and his or her imagination to portray it, we may have a work of art.

Unlike the photographs we have looked at, most photographs are not works of art. They are illustrations (45, 46), recording an event or telling a story. They may tell it well, and they may even be of beautiful subjects, but that doesn't turn them into art. To become art, they must have something more, some emotion added by the photographer that delights us or reveals some of the magic of the world in which we live.

Fifth Avenue Houses helps us to understand the difference between illustration and art by describing more than what the buildings look like. It reveals their natures—quiet, solid, and aloof—and it does this with great power. That power carries *Fifth Avenue Houses* into art.

45

When looking at a photograph, we might ask how we can tell when one work of art is superior to another. It is not an easy thing to do. We must use our eyes and our feelings to make decisions about quality. If a painting or a photograph is harmonious and raises our spirits, or even makes us think in a new way about what we are seeing, we may feel that it is a work of art. But that's not the end of the story. Quality has many levels, and we can learn about them by looking at art and reading about it. As we do, we will develop discrimination—the sense that some things have more emotional strength or beauty than others. This can be a journey without an end.

46

47

USEFUL THINGS

This chair was designed about 1927 by a
German architect named Ludwig Mies van
der Rohe (47). It is called the MR chair
and is famous the world over. The MR chair helps
us understand how some things we find in our
daily lives qualify as art.

Mies van der Rohe wanted it to remind us of
modern engineering, and so he designed the

chair to be of cane woven onto a long steel tube that was bent into a cantilever. This means that it hangs out over space without a set of rear legs to help support it. He also wanted the chair to express its function—the job it was supposed to do—so he eliminated all but the most essential parts. When the MR chair appeared, the world had never seen anything quite like it. It was a piece of geometry that you could sit on. The MR is not difficult to manufacture, and thousands like it have been produced.

What will people think of the MR chair in the years to come? Taste is forever changing, but, sooner or later, people rediscover the beauty in things that best describe past times. They become classics, and if the MR chair is not already a classic, it seems certain to become one in the future.

If you wonder about this, think about steam engines (48, 49). They look classic to us. Though

48

50

51

they changed a great deal over the years and for a while may even have seemed dull or ordinary, today we find raw beauty in them. They are fierce machines whose every part describes their function.

We could say much the same thing about great passenger liners and naval vessels. Nations have always taken pride in them, and whether they are the old R.M.S. *Queen Elizabeth* (50) or the sailing frigate U.S.S. *Constitution* (51), today we find a gracefulness in them that is timeless. And, of course, many automobiles (52), even simple ones, have a functional beauty whose appeal is bound to last.

76

The things that we have looked at so far in this chapter describe their function as well as their times. That is part of their attraction. But not every classic object describes its function. This is the Modern Diner in Pawtucket, Rhode Island (53). It is a prefabricated restaurant manufactured in 1940 under the name Sterling Streamliner. In the 1930s, during the Great Depression, the world welcomed a style that lifted people's spirits. Its name was Art Deco, but it was often called "modernistic" or "streamlined." It was used on everything from wristwatches to radios (54, 55) to diners. It was breezy and light and reminded people of speed. Things were shaped and painted in such a way that they seemed ready to roar into the future. Wristwatches and roadside diners don't race away, of course, but their design became a symbol of the world's hope for a speedy trip to better days. When those days came, other styles

54

55

replaced Art Deco. In time, though, people looked back and realized that those playful streamlined objects had joined the history of forms that we call art.

While we are looking at useful objects, we should consider a group called the craft arts. Such things as weaving, pottery, and woodworking belong to it. They come from old traditions, many of which have hardly changed over the centuries. Ponchos woven in the mountains of Peru (56) repeat the colors and designs of past ages. Copper is still beaten into bold vessels in the Turkish bazaar at Diyarbakir (57) as it has been for centuries.

56

58

59

Traditional fences as delicate as this one at Katsura Villa in Kyoto are still woven in Japan (58), and the great urns designed centuries ago for the Forbidden City in Beijing (59) are made to this day in the workshops of China. Iron is hammered into handsome shapes the world over. Those in this 175-year-old fence at Laval University in Quebec City in Quebec, Canada (60), show us the delicate rhythms that can be created from so harsh a material. In each of these objects we find ideas about beauty to which time has given dignity. As we come to understand them, they gain our deep respect.

There are also contemporary crafts. Some no longer have a function; like painting or sculpture, they're only to be looked at. But let's consider two examples of contemporary crafts that are useful and show some connection with the past.

60

61

The first is a stoneware vase made by an American craftsperson, Warren MacKenzie (61). In preparing his design, MacKenzie had old Japanese forms in mind, bowls and vases that have been made for hundreds of years. His vase has a firm, traditional shape and was made to be used. It invites us to pick it up, run our hands over the hard glaze and rough clay, feel its low ridges and powerful neck. The more we handle a piece such as this, the more we appreciate it.

This is another example of modern crafts, a large shallow stoneware bowl by another American potter, Paul Heroux (62). In it we see a field of color supported by a simple shape, a shape that bows to the quiet forms of ancient Chinese vessels. These objects show us that contemporary craftspeople draw from many sources as they work on the problems of color, texture, and shape, as all artists have done throughout the ages.

62

63

TOWNS AND CITIES

This is a view, across winter fields, of the Shaker village at Sabbathday Lake, Maine (63). Walking along its streets, we find simple white buildings, a few barns or sheds, and a large red brick dwelling house. These modest buildings were built over a period of many years, and only one or two are truly handsome. Yet

64

65

they, and the fields around them, have become a serene work of art. Throughout the village there is a feeling of thrift, the feeling that everything was built as well as it could have been built to do its job, without waste (64). It makes those rows of white buildings into a community, makes them belong to one another. That thrift organizes the village into a single harmonious whole.

The English city of Bath is more elaborate than the Shaker village, but it too is a harmonious whole. Its parade of regular forms—rows of stone buildings assembled into stately squares (65), crescents, and even a circle (66, 67) marching slowly up a set of gentle hills—and its color, which reminds us of ripe lemons, create a dignified and elegant spectacle. That softly colored parade turns Bath into a work of art.

The buildings at the Shaker village (68) look very much like one another; so do the buildings at Bath. Each community was built in a short time—Bath in a hundred years, the Shaker village in less—and each has followed the style of the years in which it was young. That loyalty to a single style is an important part of their attraction.

67

68

We might say the same thing about the white villages of Oia and Casares, the fortress town of Jaisalmer, and even the rough hamlets of Khunde and Khuri. None were built in a short time, but their buildings have followed ideas that have been handed down from century to century.

Oia's thick-walled houses perch atop the Greek island of Santorini (69, 70). They look as though they were poured from one gigantic mold to create a landscape made of tiny arcs, rectangles, and squares.

69

70

91

71

The Spanish hill town of Casares (71) is not far from the coast of Africa. Over the centuries, its simple white boxes, trooping up the steep mountain slopes, have created a giant abstract composition (72). Geometry and color unite the buildings of each of these communities and tie them to one another.

72

The Indian town of Jaisalmer is heroic poetry in pink and yellow stone (73). The blunt shapes in this stronghold—once a stop on the ancient Silk Route that led from China to Europe—repeat themselves again and again with great vigor. Jaisalmer's harmony is quite unlike the refinement of Bath or the sparkle of Casares. Here we see a community using the strength of its forms to declare its power to the world.

73

The stone village of Khunde (74), high in the Himalaya Mountains of Nepal, and the mud village of Khuri (75), in a great desert in India, both show the quiet, communal beauty that can be created with the humblest of materials and a simple, consistent style.

It is not difficult to think of the towns and villages that we have looked at as works of art. But what about large cities? Let us consider whether places that are made of all kinds of materials, show many styles of architecture, and create complicated feelings within us can be art.

74

76

77

Unlike simpler, smaller communities, a large city has many elements working with one another in complicated ways that give the city a restless appeal. For large cities *are* restless. Made of many ingredients and subject to many forces, a city is an ever-changing event that has no equal. Like Alexander Calder's mobile (22, 23), each of them is kinetic, forever on the move. They are dappled by light, sprinkled with reflections, such as these in Manhattan (76–78), and touched in a thousand other ways that give them energy. As

79

we move through large cities, there is always something more to see at the next corner, at the top of the hill, or along the river. Images follow one another as streets open into squares, as they do at Victoria Terminal in Bombay, India (79); as walls keep us out or hold us in, as these do in Bangkok, Thailand (80); or as signs such as this in Kyoto, Japan (81), light up the night. Added

80

82

to this mixture are many kinds of rhythm, some
formed by streets repeating themselves block
after block (82), some by great skylines soaring
and dipping like wild music (83), and some by
neighborhood skylines scrambling upward

83

toward the skyscrapers (84). The visual complexities that weave through every city help turn a giant like New York into a work of art that is a wonder of the world.

While large cities do not have the simple, pleasant harmonies of places like Casares or Khuri, their complicated elements and their intense, almost chaotic, energy stir our emotions in much the same way that other art does. In cities large and small—as in painting and sculpture—if we will only look, we will find that art waits to delight us. If we allow it, it will set our thoughts ablaze. It will light our dreams, instruct us, and carry us to moments so magical that they will make our hearts leap. All we have to do is want it to happen.

84

If you would like more information about the works of art in this book, here is a short list:

(1) King Zoser (2630–2611 B.C.) ruled Egypt in the Early Dynastic Period (3050–2575 B.C.). His Step Pyramid is 197 feet (60 meters) high, and its base measures 459 feet × 387 feet (139.9 meters × 118 meters). Saqqara—an ancient cemetery—is the oldest stone complex in the world, and the pyramid is its outstanding feature.

(2) This is another view of the Step Pyramid.

(3) The pyramid on the left is the Pyramid of King Chephren (2520–2494 B.C.), whom the Egyptians called Khafre. The pyramid is 471 feet (143.6 meters) high, and each side of its base is 707 feet 9 inches (215.7 meters) long. The pyramid on the right is the Pyramid of King Mycerinus (2490–2472 B.C.). The Egyptians called him Menkaure. His pyramid is 356 feet (108.5 meters) long and 218 feet (66.4 meters) high.

(4) This is the Pyramid of King Cheops (2551–2528 B.C.). Because of its size, it is often called the Great Pyramid. It is 481 feet 5 inches (146.8 meters) high, and each side of its base measures 754 feet (229.8 meters). Cheops was known to the Egyptians as Khufu.

(5) At sunset, the Pyramid of Chephren acts as a beacon, guiding travelers from the desert toward the river Nile and Cairo.

(6) The glass pyramid at the Louvre Palace is a complicated piece of engineering. It is 71 feet (21.6 meters) high, and its base measures 116 feet (35.4 meters) along each side. The building in the background, the Pavillon de Richelieu, was built in the reign of Emperor Napoleon III (1852–1870).

(7) This is a view of the Pyramid of Khafre just before sunrise.

(8) This photograph was taken of the Pyramid of Khufu as the sun was rising.

(9) According to tradition, the Horse of Selene and the other figures were carved by a sculptor named Phidias. It is more likely, however, that they were carved by several master artists working in the years 440–432 B.C. The horse is 41 inches (104.1 centimeters) high.

(10) The right profile of the Horse of Selene is shown in this photograph.

(11) The Parthenon was built in **447–432** B.C. Dedicated to Athena, the goddess of wisdom, it is the highest achievement of ancient Greek architecture.

(12) These are figures of two goddesses called the Fates. The Horse of Selene once stood next to the figure in the foreground, filling in the low corner of the pediment.

(13) The figure at right is from the Parthenon pediment and is Iris, goddess of the rainbow.

(14) This is another view of the Parthenon group.

(15) This Kota figure is 21¾ inches (55.2 centimeters) high and is thought to represent the female spirit in the world.

(16) This is called a kachina figure. It was carved from cottonwood by the Hopi, Native Americans who live in Arizona. A kachina is a supernatural spirit, and figures representing kachinas are given to Hopi children as an aid in learning about religion. This figure measures 22¾ inches × 8½ inches (57.8 centimeters × 21.6 centimeters).

(17) Jacques Lipchitz (1891–1973) was a prominent sculptor who worked in Paris and later in America. Much of his sculpture is called *Cubist*. Early in the twentieth century that name was given to a group of painters living in Paris who pioneered in showing their subjects in an abstract way. However, in Lipchitz's sculpture, the term means that bold geometric shapes are substituted for parts of the human body. *Figure* was created in Paris and is 7 feet 1¼ inches (216.5 centimeters) high.

(18) Sir Henry Moore (1898–1986) was the most prominent English artist of the twentieth century. From his studio at Much Hadham, Hertfordshire, he produced abstract forms carved in wood and stone or cast in bronze that have found their way into museums and great public buildings throughout the world. *Knife Edge Mirror Two Piece* was completed in 1978 and measures 17 feet 6½ inches × 23 feet 8 inches × 11 feet 11 inches (5.35 meters × 7.21 meters × 3.63 meters).

(19) Leonard Baskin (1922–2000), who lived in Leeds, Massachusetts, was a distinguished sculptor, draftsman, printmaker, book designer, and printer. *Homage* was made in 1970 and measures 23½ inches × 14 inches (59.7 centimeters × 35.6 centimeters).

(20) Augustus Saint-Gaudens (1848–1907) was a master American realist sculptor. He worked from studios in Rome, New York, and Cornish, New Hampshire. The $20 gold piece that he designed for the U.S. Mint in 1907 (known as the Saint-Gaudens Double Eagle) is the most majestic

American coin. The *Memorial for Admiral David Glasgow Farragut* at Madison Square Park (1878–1881) in New York City and the *Adams Memorial* at Rock Creek Cemetery (1886–1891) in Washington, D.C., are well-known examples of his work. The *Shaw Memorial,* which was commissioned by a committee of prominent Massachusetts citizens, is 11 feet × 14 feet (3.35 meters × 4.27 meters).

(21) This is a view of the full *Shaw Memorial.* The mounted figure portrays Colonel Robert Gould Shaw.

(22) While Alexander Calder (1898–1976) was not the first artist to construct kinetic (moving) sculpture, he made it famous. His mobiles and their cousins—his nonmoving *stabiles*—have become universal symbols of twentieth-century American art. This untitled work made of aluminum and steel measures 29 feet 10½ inches × 76 feet (9.1 meters × 23.16 meters).

(23) This is another view of the Calder mobile, which is at the National Gallery of Art in Washington, D.C.

(24) Piet Mondrian (1872–1944) was a Dutch painter who worked in both Paris and New York. His severe, elegant paintings are made up of strict horizontal and vertical lines that separate small fields of primary color. *Broadway Boogie-Woogie* is an oil on canvas and measures 50 inches × 50 inches (127 centimeters × 127 centimeters).

(25) Andrea del Castagno (about 1423–57) painted in Florence, Italy, during what is called the *Early Renaissance.* In the paintings of the Middle Ages, before del Castagno's time, people in art were anonymous—one person looked pretty much like the next person. However, during the Early Renaissance, painters such as del Castagno learned to show people as individuals, and it became fashionable for wealthy men and women to have their portraits painted. *Portrait of a Man* measures 21¼ inches × 15⅞ inches (54 centimeters × 40.3 centimeters).

(26) Jan Vermeer (1632–75) painted scenes from everyday life in his native city, Delft, Holland. Unlike *The Girl with the Red Hat,* most of his paintings—there are fewer than forty—are set in homes and show the quiet dignity of domestic life. *The Girl with the Red Hat* measures 9⅛ inches × 7⅛ inches (23.2 centimeters × 18.1 centimeters).

(27) Thomas Eakins (1844–1916) was one of the greatest of American painters. Whether recording outdoor life or painting portraits, he treated his subjects gently, but with a frankness and honesty that looked deeply into their natures. The *Biglin* painting measures 24⅜ inches × 16 inches (61.9 centimeters × 40.6 centimeters).

(28) William Bailey (1930–   ) is a leading painter in a movement called *New Realism.* Its members paint portraits, still lifes, and landscapes in the grand tradition of painters who worked from the Early Renaissance to the first decades of the twentieth century. Shaping the objects in his paintings through soft colors, highlights, and shadows, Bailey follows the traditions of Renaissance Italian painting. His work *Still Life—Siena Rose* is 36 inches × 30 inches (91.4 centimeters × 76.2 centimeters). William Bailey teaches art at Yale University.

(29) Milton Avery's paintings are quiet, poetic, and made of simple areas of beautiful color. Milton Avery (1893–1965) lived in New York City but often painted in New England and abroad. His *Portrait of Marsden Hartley* measures 36 inches × 28 inches (91.4 centimeters × 71.1 centimeters).

(30) Paul Gauguin (1848–1903), along with Vincent van Gogh (1853–90) and Paul Cézanne (1839–1906), is called a *Post-Impressionist.* He led a stormy life that took him from his native France to the South Seas island of Tahiti. *Fatata te Miti* measures 26¾ inches × 36 inches (67.9 centimeters × 91.4 centimeters).

(31, 32) Claude Monet (1840–1926) is the most famous of the *Impressionists*—French painters of the latter part of the nineteenth century. At times, the Impressionists used color to create a feeling of air and light—an atmosphere—so dazzling that the forms on their canvases seem to be woven from it. At other times, as in *Palazzo da Mula, Venice* (which measures 24½ inches × 31⅞ inches [62.2 centimeters × 81 centimeters]), they used somber colors to build form. In *The Houses of Parliament, Sunset,* Monet shows that deep hazy colors can serve the same purpose. The dimensions of that painting are 32 inches × 36⅜ inches (81.3 centimeters × 92.5 centimeters). In all of his paintings, form seems to be on the move, ready to change as soon as the light that colors it changes. Monet's home at Giverny, near Paris, has become a place of pilgrimage for persons who admire his soft, atmospheric pictures.

(33) Francesco Guardi (1712–93) caught the sad beauty of Venice's last days as an independent republic. His dreamlike pictures of canals and grizzled buildings show us a dying state. Four years after his death, Venice fell to Napoleon. *View on the Cannaregio, Venice* measures 18¾ inches × 29¼ inches (47.6 centimeters × 74.3 centimeters).

(34) The dimensions of *A Seaport and Classic Ruins in Italy* are 48 inches × 70 inches (121.9 centimeters × 177.8 centimeters).

(35) Fitz Hugh Lane (1804–65) painted the New

England coast and the harbors of the Northeast in the years before the Civil War. He is often called a *Luminist* because he was able to capture light when it was clear and touched with color and then use it to cast the scene as a gentle dream. Lane's *Owl's Head* measures 16 inches × 26 inches (40.6 centimeters × 66 centimeters).

(36) Marsden Hartley's (1877–1943) paintings of the Maine coast done between 1936 and the time of his death are one of the great achievements in American art. Simple, almost primitive, they express the strength of the rocky land, the forces that shaped it, and the people who live in it. Hartley, who was born in Lewiston, Maine, and died in Ellsworth, Maine, also painted in France, Germany, and the American Southwest. *After the Storm, Vinalhaven* measures 22¼ inches × 28¼ inches (56.5 centimeters × 71.8 centimeters).

(37) April Gornik (1953–   ), like Fitz Hugh Lane, is an American landscape painter who uses light and atmosphere to give her pictures a dreamy quality. But her landscapes are imaginary ones, created from dreams, scenes she remembers, photographs, and things she has made up. They are mysterious and beautiful. *Fresh Light* measures 74 inches × 96 inches (188 centimeters × 243.8 centimeters). April Gornik lives in New York City.

(38) Ellen Phelan (1943–   ) uses brilliant color

and bold strokes of a brush to form abstract landscapes. *After Atget* is 67½ inches × 87½ inches (171.45 centimeters × 222.25 centimeters). She lives and works in New York City and Westport, New York.

(39) This is a reproduction of one of Atget's photographs. It is called *Sceaux, Juin, h. matin* and shows an old road, perhaps in a park, in the town of Sceaux, which is about 6 miles from Paris. The print measures 9⅜ inches × 7 inches (23.8 centimeters × 17.8 centimeters).

(40) In a work such as *Chocorua II,* Frank Stella (1936–   ) asks us to think of a painting as an object, as we do sculpture, instead of as a picture of some real place. This idea is unusual, and so he gives the canvas an unusual shape to notify us that he is asking something special of us. *Chocorua II* measures 120 inches × 128 inches (304.8 centimeters × 325.1 centimeters).

(41) Jackson Pollock (1912–56) was one of the most influential American artists of all time. The forms on his canvases have deep rhythms, rhythms that were created by vigorously pouring and spattering paint. Pollock's style of painting is called *Abstract Expressionism*. This work, *Composition with Pouring II,* measures 25⅛ inches × 22⅛ inches (63.8 centimeters × 56.2 centimeters).

(42) Berenice Abbott (1898–1992) took up photography in Paris, where she lived from 1921 to 1929. Many of the portraits she made of artists and writers working in Paris at that time are world-famous. In 1929, she moved her studio to New York and began a series of photographs of Manhattan that are one of the finest studies of a city ever made. Ms. Abbott moved to Blanchard Township, Maine, in 1966, where she resided until her death.

(43) Mario Giacomelli (1925–2000) lived in Senigallia, Italy, where *Pretini 63* was taken. The word *pretini* means little priests, and *63* refers to the year the image was made.

(44) Harry Callahan's subjects were often everyday street scenes, but he composed the people and buildings into strong patterns that had a clear, rigorous spirit. Harry Callahan (1912–1999) began his career as a photographer in 1941 and taught at Illinois Institute of Technology and Rhode Island School of Design. His photographs are known the world over. He lived in Providence, Rhode Island.

(45) This is a view of the Taj Mahal in Agra, India. It was built by Emperor Shah Jahan in memory of his wife, Mumtaz Mahal. The Taj Mahal was designed by a Persian architect named Isa Khan. Construction of the white marble building began in 1631 and continued until 1653.

(46) This is a view of King's College Chapel at Cambridge University in Cambridge, England, as you would see it from the banks of the Cam River. The chapel's ceiling—in a style called *fan vaulting*—was a gift from King Henry VIII and is famous throughout the world. The low building on the left is the Clare College Library.

(47) Mies van der Rohe's MR chair was first made in 1926. The manufacturer was the Joseph Muller Berliner Metallgewerbe of Berlin, Germany. One of the most influential architects of the twentieth century, Ludwig Mies van der Rohe (1886–1969) was once director of the Bauhaus, a famous architectural school in Dessau, Germany. He came to the United States in 1938 to become director of the department of architecture of Illinois Institute of Technology, in Chicago.

(48) Steam engines such as this have climbed Mount Washington in New Hampshire since 1869. At 6,288 feet, the mountain is the highest in the Northeast, and its cog railway carries passengers up the steepest rail grades in the world. Because the grades are so steep, the engine's boiler is installed at an angle so that it will be horizontal on the sharp rises.

(49) This steam train carried passengers and freight through the Andean valleys of Peru for many years.

(50) The Royal Mail Ship *Queen Elizabeth* was built by John Brown & Co. Ltd. in Glasgow, Scotland. It was launched in 1938; its 83,673 gross tons made it the largest vessel in the world. The *Queen Elizabeth* was used as a troop transport during World War II. It was retired as a passenger liner in 1968, and in 1972, while in Hong Kong, it burned and sank.

(51) The U.S.S. *Constitution* was designed in 1794 by Joshua Humphreys of Philadelphia and built by Hartt's Shipyard in Boston, Massachusetts. The ship, nicknamed *Old Ironsides,* is a frigate—a fast, heavily armed ship—and is still a commissioned vessel in the U.S. Navy.

(52) This automobile is called a Karmann Ghia and was produced in Osnabrück, Germany, from 1956 to 1975. The body was designed by Luigi Segre of the Ghia Company of Turin, Italy, and was built by Karmann Coach Works. The car itself was manufactured by Volkswagen A.G.

(53) The Modern Diner is located at 364 East Avenue in Pawtucket, Rhode Island. It was built in 1940 by the Sterling Dining Car Co. in Merrimac, Massachusetts, a firm that once made special streamlined bodies for such classic automobiles as Packard and Duesenberg.

(54) This radio was manufactured by Motorola beginning in the year 1940. It is called *Model 50XC* and it is 9⅝ inches (24.4 centimeters) long, 5¾ inches (14.6 centimeters) tall, and 5⅛ inches (13 centimeters) deep.

(55) The manufacturing of this radio began in 1939. The producer was the Sparton Radio Company, and the model is called *Cloisonné.* It measures 8 inches (20.3 centimeters) long, 5⅜ inches (13.7 centimeters) tall, and 4⅜ inches (11.1 centimeters) deep.

(56) For centuries, ponchos have been traditional outer garments worn by the native peoples of Mexico, Ecuador, Peru, and Bolivia.

(57) Diyarbakir, on the banks of the Tigris River in southeastern Turkey, was founded about 1500 B.C. Over the centuries, its ancient bazaar has been a trading center for Assyrians, Persians, Greeks, Romans, Arabs, Ottomans, and Kurds.

(58) Katsura Imperial Villa in Kyoto was completed around 1636. It was built for a royal prince, and its simple, elegant design and perfect workmanship make it an outstanding example of traditional Japanese architecture.

(59) The Forbidden City is in the heart of Beijing and was the fortified palace of China's emperors from about 1406 to 1911.

(60) The building in the background is the Séminaire de Québec, founded in 1663 by François de Montmorency Laval.

(61) Warren MacKenzie's pottery is simple and natural and is made with great feeling for the soft, easily shaped nature of clay—qualities that are also found in ancient Japanese and Korean ceramics. These qualities link Mr. MacKenzie (1924–   ) to two legendary potters, Shoji Hamada of Japan and Bernard Leach of the United Kingdom, each of whom honored the old Oriental traditions. Warren MacKenzie lives in Stillwater, Minnesota.

(62) The designs on the surface of Paul Heroux's piece show us that some contemporary potters— now called *ceramic artists*—wish to merge their work with the arts of painting and sculpture. Paul Heroux (1946–   ) lives in New Gloucester, Maine.

(63) The land of the Sabbathday Lake Shaker village rises from a point near a bog, moves upward through a series of old fields, passes the settlement, and ends at a great crest crowned with apple trees. This Shaker community was established in 1793 and is the only remaining active community of a once thriving American sect.

(64) The Sabbathday Lake Shaker building on the left is the 1794 Meetinghouse. The building on the right is the Ministry's Shop.

(65) The Abbey Churchyard is in the center of the oldest part of Bath. People have used it as a place to gather since the sixteenth century, and probably before.

(66) The King's Circus was designed by Bath's principal architect, John Wood the elder. It was begun in 1754 and is divided into three sections, each of which has eleven houses. It is one of the great sights of a remarkable city.

(67) This is another view of the King's Circus.

(68) This is another view of the Sabbathday Lake Shaker village. The Boy's Shop is on the left; the Spin Shop is on the right.

(69) This is a view of Oia from Thíra.

(70) Oia is a small white village located to the south of Thíra, Santorini's principal town.

(71) Casares's streets are narrow, steep, and spotless.

(72) This is a visitor's first glimpse of Casares.

(73) Jaisalmer is in the Thar Desert in the western part of Rajasthan. It was founded in 1156. In the days of caravans, it was a trading center for wool, hides, camels, and sheep.

(74) The elevation of Khunde is about 11,000 feet. It overlooks the Khumbu Valley, a main route to the base of Mt. Everest.

(75) Khuri is a simple desert village close to India's border with Pakistan. Its mud-walled, thatched-roof buildings are often decorated with bold geometric designs.

(76) These buildings form a long glass wall along the west side of Avenue of the Americas in midtown Manhattan, New York City.

(77) The Solomon R. Guggenheim Museum was designed by the most famous American architect of the twentieth century, Frank Lloyd Wright. It was finished in 1959 and sits on New York's Fifth Avenue between 88th Street and 89th Street. Spiraling its way into the sky, it is one of the most wonderful modern buildings in existence.

(78) This is a view of a part of the north side of West 55th Street in Manhattan, New York City.

(79) Victoria Terminal, a railroad station named for Queen Victoria of England, was built in the late nineteenth century. Its ornate style, called *Victorian,* was very popular throughout the British Empire during Queen Victoria's sixty-year reign.

(80) This is a view of Jetuphon Road next to Wat Pho, the oldest and largest temple in Bangkok.

(81) This is a pachinko parlor in Kyoto. Pachinko is a type of pinball game that is very popular in Japan. Pachinko parlors are famous for their bright, gaudy lighting and blaring music.

(82) This is a view of 54th Street west of Avenue of the Americas in Manhattan.

(83) This is a view of the West Side of Manhattan, looking south from a point near Lincoln Center.

(84) This view of the east side of the southern tip of Manhattan was taken from the top of one of the towers of the World Trade Center. It shows the East River and the Brooklyn Bridge (right) and the Manhattan Bridge (left).

Page numbers in **boldface** refer to illustrations.

ABOUT THE AUTHOR

Philip M. Isaacson was an attorney and the art critic for the *Maine Sunday Telegram*. His first book for young readers was the award-winning introduction to architecture *Round Buildings, Square Buildings, & Buildings That Wiggle Like a Fish*.

Mr. Isaacson passed away in 2013.